# ZERO TO $100K!

# ZERO TO $100K!

## THE COMPLETE GUIDE ON HOW TO START A SUCCESSFUL LAWN CARE COMPANY

BRIAN FULLERTON

# Zero To $100k!

Brian Fullerton

*www.LawntrepreneurAcademy.com*

# Contents

# Dedication

I want to dedicate this book to the hundreds of thousands of fans, readers, listeners, and friends across the globe to the Brian's Lawn Maintenance community. What an incredible journey it's been over the last few years. I am incredibly grateful for the impact you've had on my life and, hopefully, the impact I've been able to make on yours. I'd also like to take a minute and dedicate this book to my wife, Elizabeth Fullerton. Her encouragement and love have made me who I am today. I would be nothing without her. Together, there isn't anything we cannot accomplish, babe. I love you! Thank you for always supporting me and joining me on this wild adventure called life.

# Introduction

I know what you're thinking because it's the same thought I would've had if I was picking up a book like this for the first time. Do we need another success book about "How To Start An XYZ Business," sharing the Xs and Os, about how to start or run a business? You're right, probably not. The bookshelves are jam-packed with books like that! Second thought: A book about how to start a lawn care business? Lame! How difficult could it be!

I mean, isn't it all just about making tall grass short? Excellent point, fair enough! But this book is so much more than that. Let me explain.

In this book, I want to share the adventure that has been the last 20 years of my life, from starting from scratch with a green industry business, coming from absolutely nothing, and making something out of ourselves today. We didn't start our business with any silver spoon in our mouths. We had no connections, contacts, or education on the green industry! If I can be honest, the first 11 years were abysmal! There wasn't anything I would've been excited to share because my wife and I were flat-broke! Our business was a joke; our equipment looked like it came from a junkyard, oh yeah, and profit? Never heard of it!

I want to take you on an adventure with me, one with parallel paths. The first is our story about starting, growing, and building a successful lawn care company. The other course is about our journey to becoming successful Lawntrepreneurs. We won't get super heavy into the motivational side of things, but I want to let you know that if we can do it, you can do it. Starting your own business doesn't have to be a decade of trial and error like it was for me.

My goal is that by the time we're done with this journey, I can help you understand that even with limited finances, limited education, dedication, and a strong work ethic, you can start and grow a thriving green industry business. I know you can because we did, and you can too. I promise you, it won't happen overnight, but you can build something over the next 3-5 years that you can be proud of. In 5-10 years, you can create something that others will recognize and be proud of. And in 10-20 years, well, really, the sky's the limit, and that's totally up to you with where you want to take things!

You see, my first ten years in business were anything but a success. We struggled with almost every area of the company, from picking the right equipment to building our routes, how we added customers, and so much more. Nothing worked correctly, we needed a vision for the company, and we were throwing mud up on the wall to see what would stick. Not exactly a recipe for success, as you would imagine.

Fast forward the last five years. With tremendous help from the social media lawn care community, my friend Michael, and so many more, we righted our ship and finally made some significant headway. It wasn't all sunshine and rainbows, but through the good and bad days (which we'll share!), we got our business to a respectful size and made enough profit to take care of our family with dignity. Self-employment isn't for the faint of heart! But I will say this: I would take the worst day of being self-employed any day over the best day of working for someone else. That's a fact.

I hope my story shows that even if you don't have a silver-spoon upbringing or all of the right connections, you can still make it happen for yourself. The green industry is a respectable industry to participate in, and a lawn and landscaping business can help you build a dream life for which you can be excited! It won't happen overnight, but within a few short years, you can create an incredible company that you and your team can be proud of.

Each chapter we share will take you on parallel paths of how I started and built my lawn & landscaping business, and the key takeaways and helpful tips to help you maximize the launch of your company. I'll do my best to spell out the marching orders step by step, in case you're simply looking for the "How To's" and "X's and O's" of starting your company. I hope that our ceiling can be your floor, and we can help clear the fog about the initial steps you need to take to start your business.

Through this journey, I want to help you lay the foundations to start, grow and run a successful lawn care business and help you achieve what I believe to be the first milestone: starting from scratch and earning $100k in revenue. That is the first accurate benchmark in business and can begin to support you and your family financially. From there, it is entirely up to you, but let's start by laying the foundation and launching your business over the next 12-24 months and setting yourself up for success.

Let us begin this journey together.

# Chapter One

# My Baywatch Moment

I remember it like it was yesterday, the moment in my life when everything changed. I was out in Canton, Michigan fertilizing lawns for the chemical company I was working for, zoned out, going through the motions, and making my rounds on my route. I remember it being a brutally hot day, the heat had to be in the 90s, and the humidity made it almost unbearable to work. I had just pulled up curbside on my next stop, ready to hop out, spray the lawn, and eradicate any pesky weeds, just like I've done thousands of times before. I remember reaching down to switch on the pump on the Isuzu cab-over truck, but just then, a pickup truck pulled across from me, catching my attention.

Two young guys in their 20s jumped out of their truck, wearing basketball shorts and cut-off T-Shirts, one wearing headphones and the other with earmuffs. "What was this?" I thought to myself. I vividly remember time slowing down, and these guys began to move in slow motion. As they dropped the trailer ramp gate, one hopped on the lawn mower, and another started the weed whip. They were about to mow the lawn to my left while I tackled the property to my right. I couldn't stop but stare and watch in amazement at these two young guys mowing grass, working synchronously, a beautiful tandem tapestry on display. I often refer to it as my Baywatch Moment because I couldn't stop staring at these two guys, what I perceived to be living the dream, mowing grass on a beautiful summer day without a care.

I immediately started thinking to myself, here I am in long pants, a long sleeve shirt, and rubber boots, putting on slimy wet rubber gloves, basking in a tanker truck with no air conditioning. The fertilizer truck had an indescribable grotesque musk that would've made a gym locker room blush, melting away for a paltry $11.50 an hour. I imagined these guys were getting at least $25 to mow this property in the same 15 minutes it took me to fertilize the neighbor's lawn. They finished cutting, trimming, and blowing this property without a sweat. Now to add insult to injury, they chugged down a Gatorade bottle, hopped in their truck, and off to the next property. You could tell they enjoyed and took pride in what they did. Time snapped back into reality, the whimsical slow motion had ended, and I immediately thought to myself, "what am I doing with my life"? I can do that! Hell, I used to do that!

You see, that was me not that long ago! When I was ten years old until I was about 16, I mowed lawns just like those two guys did, albeit not in slow motion like a Baywatch rerun. I remember when I was a young teenager, with my lawn care business back in my mom's trailer park push-mowing lawns for $13 a yard. I loved it! I enjoyed the fresh air, the semi-permanent farmer's tan, and the exercise. I was truly living the dream. Fast forward six years. I found myself stuck inside a nasty tanker truck, spraying all kinds of chemicals that did who knows what, utterly unsatisfied with where my life had taken me. Not only did I not like the circumstances of that fertilizer job, but I didn't like the prospects of my current career path. I had zero interest in working for someone else since getting fired from my previous job 12 months prior!

I decided right then and there something had to change. I thought to myself; I used to mow grass when I was a kid; how difficult could it be now that I am an adult? Heck, half of my old customer base I still kept in touch with (after all, I was still living with my mom in the trailer park!), and they had been asking if I could help them mow their lawns on the weekends anyways! I decided right then and there, what the heck, let's do it. I am 100% getting back into lawn care. What's the worst that could happen?

Chapter Two

# If It Were Easy Then Everybody Would Do It

I've had many people over the years share their interest in starting a business of their own, from being a fitness instructor to starting a manufacturing business and, of course, a thriving lawn and landscaping business. The stories all sound very similar. They have a dream and a goal and believe they can make a difference. What I've come to find that separates those who succeed and those who only talk about it is one thing: they took action on that dream. The successful person might have had only some of the correct answers initially, but they found the right answers along the way. It's the good ole "jump off the cliff and build your airplane on the way down," idiom as my friend Josh Latimer says.

You see, what I didn't know back in the day was a lot! I needed to learn how to start a business. I wanted to know what a FEIN was, or an LLC, or what a bookkeeper did. I needed to learn about quarterly taxes, 1099s, payroll, etc. After all, who teaches you this stuff? I was fresh out of school, and for someone who had perfect attendance for the last four years in high school, I promise you this: they didn't teach us a darn thing about success OR how to run a successful business. All they taught us was that college was the ticket. I know; I was there every single day!

When I started a lawn care business, I thought about what most people do: get a lawn mower, get a string trimmer, get some flyers, and mow the grass! After all, how difficult could it be? Everyone has a neighbor, brother, or co-worker that mows a few lawns on the side, am I right? That was my approach! And it worked! Well, for a little while, that is. But it didn't truly set me up for success. Let me explain.

When I got back into lawn care, I thought all I had to do was contact my old customers and let them know I was back in the lawn care business. I figured I would get the previous 10-15 customers back that I previously had, track them on an excel file on my netbook (remember those?), and that was it! I would be hog nasty rich! Unfortunately, that's different from how it went down.

My back-end office and accounting could have been better, and so was my equipment! It had been 5+ years since I fired any of it up, including the trimmers and blowers. I remember my first round of flyers; they were so pathetic! I had five paragraphs titled "Who, What, When, Where & Why," explaining my new business. I later found the template 15 years later in an email, and let's say it's a miracle that we've made it this far.

I was stitching together the best information and building this Frankenstein business from the ground up. As I've said before, lawn care & landscaping is one of the most simple businesses, but it's shocking how many people screw it up. I wasn't even a month in business and was already heading down the wrong path.

Chapter Three

# Going Back To Our Roots

I wish we had tremendous success with our new enterprise right out of the gate, but that was hardly the case. We struggled with almost everything initially, from picking the correct name for the business to figuring out the right equipment to purchase and so much more. I had never really put a game plan together for the company other than taking care of some of my initial customers and making their lawns look as beautiful as possible. It was an oversimplified approach, but that's all I knew how to do from my early days of running my small business. I never really considered what I was getting myself into. I was more concerned with what I was getting myself out of, and that was a suffocating 9-5 job that I didn't enjoy or see a future in. Can anyone relate?

Back then, we didn't have access to social media like Facebook, YouTube, and Instagram to show how to do the job or training courses to help us get our feet wet. It was all trial by fire! Sure, there might've been a local business owner who had a successful company in town, but to get them to open up and share about their best practices or to give us some helpful tips to grow? Forget about it! Why would they spill the beans and create more competition in their local market? That wouldn't make sense, and I can't blame them, either! I was throwing mud up on the wall to see what would stick! Let's break down the initial few steps of starting your lawn care business, and we'll contrast it with what I did. Outside of deciding to start a business and when to go full-time (we'll cover that in a later chapter!), the first thing we had to do was come up with the name!

When I got back into lawn care, I immediately reverted to the same name I had used when I was ten to sixteen: Brian's Lawn Care. Fancy, huh? My name was Brian, and I did lawn care; what else was I missing? It wasn't the worst name I've ever heard of for a business, but it could have been better. I only spent a little time thinking about what I wanted to name this rebirthed enterprise. I was dead set on getting out of my job at the fertilizer company, and any name would've been fine with me. How we went from Brian's Lawn Care to Brian's Lawn Maintenance is a funny story worth a quick share.

I still remember entering the 1200 building in Pontiac, Michigan, and waiting for the county clerk to register my business officially. I went to the window and submitted the necessary paperwork, observing the clerk as she quickly skimmed my paperwork. After a few keystrokes on her keyboard, she shook her head in disappointment, catching me off guard. "Honey, unfortunately, that name is already registered; you're going to have to pick something else.", she said. "What do you mean? It's already been taken?" I exclaimed. "Yep - someone beat you to the punch. Can you think of something else you'd like to go with?" she said. I immediately went through the Rolodex of names in my head that I quickly considered, but before I could land on any of them, the clerk asked me "What do you do?". I told her, "I maintain lawns and mow the grass!". She nodded. "What about Brian's Lawn Maintenance?". I looked at her, and with little hesitation, I said, "Sure, let's do it!". That was the birth of our new company, the signing of our entrepreneurial declaration of independence! We had a name for our business, it was registered, and I was off to the races!

Chapter Four

# How To Pick A Great Name

One of the most common questions I get asked is, "Brian, if you had to do it all over again, what would you do differently?". Great question. Let's get into some Xs and Os and talk about a topic that I would've approached radically differently if I were to do it all over again. Let's talk about how to select a quality name for your business.

When I can share with a new business owner or someone looking to start their business relatively soon, I suggest that they take a long hard look into the future and figure out what type of business they want. After all, what is the end game? Do you want to be a small owner-operator style business, doing a few hundred thousand in revenue? If so, fantastic! What about building the next five to ten-million-dollar regional business? That sounds good to me! Do you focus on lawn maintenance, snow removal, landscaping, or hardscape and construction? The sky is the limit, but we must make sure we dial in what we want our future business to look like now.

When picking a good name for your business, a few suggestions I'd like to help make are: Choose a name that sounds highly professional. Pick a name that commands respect and sounds like an actual company, even from day one. Pick an all-inclusive name; don't single yourself out on a specific service. Lastly, pick a name that allows your business to grow into; that way, you're not pigeonholed into providing a particular service or to a specific region.

Sure, Tom's Lawn Care sounds okay if your name was Tom, but what if we changed it up a little bit? We could go with Tom's Landscaping Services; that already sounds better. But what if you plan to get out of the field one day? Your customers are expecting to see Tom there doing the work. What if we instead went with Tom's last name, Yeager, and went with Yeager Landscaping Services? That sounds a tad more professional already. Let's keep it going! One problem: Yeager Landscaping Services is potentially a little restrictive. What if we plan to get into snow and ice management down the road? Or high-end residential hardscaping? What about commercial site management? Let's see if we can work on that name a little more and have some fun with this exercise. Some great alternatives could be Yeager Property Management, Yeager Site Management, Yeager Lawn & Snow, Yaeger Outdoor Services, to name a few. Those sound way more professional and serious then Tom's Lawn Care!

The main idea here is, what type of company do you want to build? What do you want to be known for? By the way, that can change over time! However, changing your name after you've been established in your market for two, five, or even ten years can be challenging. You don't want to lose that name recognition and branding that you've spent time and money on and potentially confuse new customers or even your existing clients.

I know this might go without saying and without trying to sound harsh, but try to stay away from names that include things like: "Your First Name," "Lawn Care," "Service," "Pros," or "Bros." Some other suggestions of phrases to avoid: Descriptive names of how work is performed or cheesy names that sound more catchy than they do professional. I would take those names back to the drawing board, personally. Phrases like "Mikey Mowz," "Triple Cut Services," "A Cut Above," or "Done Right Lawn Care" are some quick examples. They're not awful by any means, but there is much room for improvement. You only get one chance to make a first impression, so let's ensure we get it right!

One other quick suggestion when picking your name is to consider the color scheme you'd like to go for with your business. If I can be honest, deciding on a color scheme and palette that works for your business, besides choosing a great name, is a must! Traditional colors like greens, yellows, whites, and grays are safe. Bold colors like Purple, Red, Yellow, and Orange could be a great idea, especially with an eye-catching design, but I advise caution. You immediately think of specific industries when you use certain colors (blue for pools, yellow and orange for roads or asphalt services, and so forth), so be sure to stick with a natural color scheme for your industry. You can break the rules, but be sure that the color you pair with is neutral, like black, white, or gray. Explore some different font types, color schemes, and names of your business. A few hours of work on the front end can save you hundreds of hours (and thousands of dollars!) on the back end years later.

Chapter Five

# Picking The Right Entity

Before we get too far ahead of ourselves and start talking about getting new customers or purchasing shiny equipment, I wanted to spend a minute on the legal aspect of starting your business. As you can imagine, I am not a lawyer, so take this advice with a grain of salt and consult with one as you start your new business. When I started business at the county clerk's office, I needed to learn the difference between an LLC, DBA, LLP, or many ways to register a business correctly. I also realized that although the county clerk helped me write my DBA that day, she wasn't necessarily there to help me select the right entity for my business long term, that wasn't her job.

Let's break things down very simply when registering your new business. In most states, filing a "DBA" means registering to "Doing Business As". If your name is Mike Johnson, fantastic, you can now do business as Johnson Property Management! After registering for your FEIN (Federal Employer ID Number), you can open a business checking account with your local bank or credit union. Customers can start paying you with checks, and you can start taking deposits or sending invoices for that business' checking account; fantastic! Ok then, so what's the issue with a DBA? The problem is that you are personally liable for your work. You see, you are now the business, and the business is now you when you're a sole proprietor. If you get into an accident with the company vehicle, you can be on the hook for the accident as the business owner and personally liable! There's no separation between you and the business. If someone tried to come after you for that accident or injury, they could sue your company and you! There are better ways to protect yourself or your assets, as you can see!

What may seem like a no-brainer to some was an eye-opening experience for me back in 2006. We realized that after our business started to pick up some steam, we had a sizable enterprise generating some decent sales. After learning from self-help books and my newly hired CPA the difference between an LLC and a DBA (think asset protection!), I panicked and immediately filed as an LLC at the State level for our business. If you want to start a new business, register directly as an LLC. It will cost you more money upfront, but it could save you from a nightmare scenario down the road. God forbid anything serious or catastrophic happens, you'll be so glad you had an extra layer of protection between you and your business.

One other quick tip, steer away from any of the expedited services you can use online to register your business and help zoom things along. Usually, those services add unnecessary markups and add-on services that later cost you hundreds of dollars more in hidden fees and add-ons. My suggestion: hire an attorney locally to help you set up your new LLC, which includes more than just submitting your paperwork and paying the small fee at the State level. There are other forms you need to file, paperwork to process, and so much more. Trust me; it'll be some of the best money you can spend right out of the gate. Hire professional help! We get paid to cut grass, not cut corners, and I often see too many people cheating out in the early stages of their business registering as a "DBA" or filing their own LLC.

# Chapter Six

# Spreading Our Wings

Now that we were back in the lawn care business, my immediate goal was to get as many new customers as fast as possible. I was on a mission to create extra income outside my 9-5. Let's face it; I also wanted to go full-time in my own business and, one day, call my own shots. That's what I saw that fateful day, staring at the two lawn workers mowing the neighbor's property while I was stuck inside that tanker truck. I knew that the dozen or so trailer park customers I picked back up from my early days as a teenager weren't going to cut it alone.

We had to get creative and start looking toward acquiring new customers, but not just any client! I wanted to start working in the nicer subdivisions of the lawns that I was familiar with because of that fertilizer job. We saw the most opportunity in the middle and upper-middle-class subdivision-style properties. The reason was simple: most of these homes had manicured lawns which were watered and fertilized regularly, and they cared about the appearance of their home! If they didn't keep the standard, their HOA was on their heels, ensuring they complied! By the way, ask me again why I prefer to live out in the country away from HOAs. Another story for another time, but I digress.

I had no problems with the customers in the trailer park where I grew up. They were all fine people. However, they had a limited budget and interest in taking care of their lawn and landscaping needs. I realized early on that if I wanted a solid flow of revenue, I would have to branch out into the more excellent areas of town and secure these beautiful properties. Sticking to the middle-class and upper-middle-class areas of town and subdivisions is an excellent area to market your business.

If you're starting your business fresh, one exercise that I'll challenge you to do is brainstorm for a few minutes about this topic: What is your ideal customer? What type of money do they spend on their property annually? Hundreds? Thousands? Or even hundreds of thousands? What are their home values? $200k? $500k? One million dollars or above? What types of services are they looking for? What types of properties do they have? Are they rural or urban? Flat land or dense forest properties? These are all questions I wish I had spent more time on when I first started my business. We call this exercise "find your ideal customer avatar."

The fun part about this exercise is that it allows you to start thinking creatively about what type of business you want to run and what services you want to offer! Do you have a knack for tree trimming? What about hardscaping and installing patios or retaining walls? These conversations will look drastically different when you look at the various home values we describe. One of the best things you can ask yourself which we mentioned earlier is: What do you want to be known for? You may become your area's premier outdoor living space installer for $2m+ homes! You may desire to be known for moderate-sized landscaping installs and renovations; that's great too. I know some folks with ten-million-dollar lawn maintenance businesses, and that's their bread and butter! The decision is entirely up to you!

This exercise will help you triangulate your marketing, name creation, and services before you set foot on the showroom floor to buy equipment or pass out your first flyer. I often return to this exercise because our business changes every year. Our skillset improves, our interests change, the market fluctuates, and we occasionally like to try new things! Please take a quick minute (or two!), brainstorm on the questions above, and see where they take you.

# Chapter Seven

# The Blitzkrieg Strategy

When marketing and getting new customers, I'm often asked what is the best approach. Do we utilize yard signs, flyers, postcards, or word of mouth? Yes! What about having a website, customer referral programs, and running Facebook ads? Yep - those too! What about investing in vehicle wraps, billboard ads, and supporting local community events or fundraisers? Again, the answer is still yes! I have a simple way to approach the conversation about getting new customers, and I call it the Blitzkrieg Strategy. It means utilizing every piece of artillery and ammo you have with overwhelming force to get in front of the customer! The reality is: it all works. But what I've found works best is when it's all done together, simultaneously. That is the surefire way to make sure you get the opportunity for that phone to ring and get that new customer.

When I started to spread my wings and get into the nicer subdivisions, I only had a little cash to reinvest in marketing. We did what we could, and where we couldn't compete in terms of quality, we made up in quantity. Do postcards work better than lawn flyers? You know it. Do vehicle wraps work better than vehicle magnets? Of course. Don't feel that you have to break the bank to get your message out there - at least not initially. You don't have to spend a fortune on your marketing. I've seen low-budget campaigns outproduce expensive marketing efforts time and time again. The secret? Frequency.

I often tell new business owners to remember to market their businesses as often as possible, not just during the spring rush. There's something to a quality marketing campaign utilizing different advertising strategies consistently over the season that can generate huge success. You don't need a huge budget to make that happen. Consistency is the key here, and continually having those soft touches and impressions on your customers has been the best way to grow your brand and generate new business. Let's briefly discuss each advertising strategy for a quick second and where to begin.

We'll break this into two categories: traditional print advertising and high-tech with social media, websites, and ads. The biggest misconception with your marketing is that it has to be expensive to get results. I don't believe that to be true. Some of the cheapest marketing I've found delivers the best results. Initially, you may start with a ten cent paper flyer explaining a little more about who you are and what your service offers, and that's a great call to action. We have a great example of the template we created on our website. Simple flyers that you fold and place on top of a mailbox flag or in the mailbox chute for advertisements can be an effortless way to get the word out about your new business quickly. We use these as a low-cost way to drum up business quickly. A quick tip: never place anything inside the mailbox; that is illegal!

An upgrade from flyers would be postcard marketing. What was the most effective form of marketing that helped our business grow in those early days? It was hiring a marketing agency to make us a quality postcard design. We would purchase around 2,500-5,000 postcards every spring and pass them out once the weather breaks. For us in Michigan, that was usually mid to late March. Once everyone experiences that first spring day when the weather is 50 degrees and people start wearing shorts and t-shirts again, that's our signal to start this marketing campaign!

The phone usually starts to ring immediately and a flood of inquiries comes in for quotes and bids. A quick tip: ensure you are ready for the influx of new calls! Be prepared to **answer**! Yes I said it, answer your phone when someone calls you over this next 5-day period! As someone who personally sends almost every call to voicemail myself, this is a time to pick up the phone! New inquiries are coming in and you must be ready to take those calls. Also, ensure that your voicemail is clear and that there is space for any additional calls you may miss. Once you cast your nets into the water, you have to be ready to reel them in!

Another great way to spread your message around town is with yard signs. These can be expensive to the new business owner, sometimes costing $10+ per sign until you find a quality volume designer where you can get that price to half of that, typically from an online merchant. Yard signs are an effective way to get new business and get the word out about a specific part of town where your company is now offering service in that location. We use yard signs at busy intersections around town, the local grocery store, and at the exits of certain HOAs where we are looking to get more business. A quick tip: put out your yard signs on Friday afternoon after the local government and city workers are gone for the week, and folks are likely to drive by them over the weekend. All too often, we've put out 5-10 yard signs around town on a Monday only to receive a call to round them all up by the city ordinance officer by Monday afternoon. Not fun, as you can imagine! One last tip: stick to a reasonable size, something like 12"x18", which gets your message across but isn't obnoxious either. We've found that to be the happy medium between marketing our business and not having them plucked out (at least initially!) from the local city office.

Vehicle and trailer wraps are my favorite ways to market your business. Although it may not be an initial marketing tactic for your business due to its price tag, wraps can be a great way to get your message out there. It's like a rolling billboard going down the street that says "Hey, look at me!". An eye-catching design that people see repetitively as your rig is zipping across town is a no-brainer strategy to get the phone to ring and add credibility and authority to your business. Let's face it, when a wrapped box truck, company vehicle, or enclosed landscape trailer pulls up, you immediately think professional, right or wrong. The sticker shock can catch you off guard sometimes, so be prepared to spend $2k-$5k for something like this, or even more. I promise you, spring for it as soon as possible. Some of our best customers (including commercial accounts!) have come from our vehicle wrap and folks "seeing our crews all over town!".

Next is having a quality website and Google My Business listing to drive leads and establish additional credibility for your company. Whenever I see a business, I first Google them and see what they're all about. I will skim the reviews and the company's photos and decide if I want more information. These days, if you are not on Google, you do not exist, period. Registering a Google My Business listing is relatively easy and free. Invest in a quality website to take your web presence to the next level. Nothing adds more credibility to your company than having a website where people can look you up and get more information about your services. When I started my business, a website would've cost me $10,000, if not more! Today you can get a quality website that helps you with that first impression for around $2,000. It's money well spent, I guarantee you. A quick tip: make the design and layout easy to navigate, and have a call to action on the front page! Refrain from burying your prospect in endless photos and testimonies about your company where they will lose interest and their attention will fade. Give them enough information to add credibility, and point them to a "Call Now" button or "Submission Form" to get more information. That's it!

The last category I wanted to touch on is where folks understand it has the most significant upside, but they give it the least amount of time and attention it deserves. I'm talking, of course, about social media. One of the most effective ways to market your business is with Facebook, Instagram, YouTube, and LinkedIn. When brainstorming your business name, check if the handles are available on these popular platforms first! If so, secure them as quickly as possible, even if you don't plan to build them out for months to come. Building out your social media pages takes time, but once they're established, all you have to do is maintain them by adding new content regularly.

You'd be surprised to learn how many people "snoop" on your business on social media before they ever pick up the phone to call you. I do it all the time! I want to see how active they are on social media and if they stay relevant with their work and services. If your last post on social media was two years ago, that makes me pump the brakes about the credibility of your business. A quick tip: how many times you post and the types of photos or work you highlight are less critical than it is with the consistency of your posting. No matter your upload frequency, pick something you can stick to! At least once a week on these platforms is a great start. Keep them active, keep them updated, make sure your links are up to date and engage with people who comment, like, and show interest in your work.

Every person starting their business will have a different approach and a different budget to work with. We started with cheap lawn flyers, vehicle magnets, and free business cards. Over time, we graduated to quality postcard designs, trailer wraps, yard signs, and websites, but it took time. The key is to keep reinvesting as much as possible for as long as possible. How we market our business today drastically differs from how we first started. If there is any one thing you're going to get good at, get good at marketing your business!

# Chapter Eight

# Building Route Density

An old saying goes, "One hand washes the other, and they both wash the face." Two items that go hand in hand with a thriving lawn and landscaping company are excellent marketing and great route density. I will say this on the record: outside of having quality pricing and knowing your numbers, having great route density and having a defined service area will be the number one thing that makes or breaks your new enterprise.

What exactly is route density, and why is it essential to spend some time on this as we grow our company? After all, isn't the idea to get as many new customers as possible? Who cares where they're located, right? Well, not exactly. One of the biggest enemies of your service business is windshield time. That is the dead space that happens in between jobs. There's no money to be made when we incur windshield time. That being said, the idea for lawn maintenance is to keep your routes as tight as possible. All in the same city, or even better, in the same subdivisions, if you can imagine! The only time we would bend this rule is if we had a more significant dollar job that we are taking care of for a customer. Think about a project north of $5,000 that may require you to be on-site for three days. Having 30-45 minutes of drive time could be worth it for a job that size. But for an average $40-$50 weekly mow client, probably not.

Where I first learned about route density and how I came to study this topic began right in my own backyard! When I got back in business, my first customers came from the trailer park where I grew up. It wasn't out of the question to mow ten trailer park lawns in an 8-hour day. As our equipment improved and we became more efficient in general, there were some days when we had to cut north of 40 plus trailer park lawns in one day! I know some people give trailer park lawns a bad rep, but hey, that's where I started! When we were getting fifteen dollars a yard and knocking out 40+ lawns in a day, that added up to some good coin! The best part about it? We didn't even have to tow the truck and trailer around to do it! Admittedly, it looked a little hillbilly zipping up and down the trailer parks, putting our string trimmer on the mower deck in tow with a backpack blower, but it worked! It was an incredibly efficient setup, and that was the birth of my realization that having great route density would be our ticket to success when it came to lawn maintenance.

When I decided to branch out of the trailer park and get into the nicer subdivisions, the very first thing we did was set boundaries for our service area. Where we live in Metro Detroit, Michigan, the roads around us are primarily divided by "mile" roads. Think 6-Mile, 7-Mile, and yes 8-Mile road! We also have a bunch of streets that run north and south, which makes for a grid effect where we live. When I took a look at a map (way before Google Earth!), I looked at the density of the homes and subdivisions in my area and drew what I will call our service area. It was a 2 square mile area, broken up by mile roads and major thoroughfares.

I know what some of you are thinking, 2 miles? Is that even possible to have a successful business operating in such a small area? Remember, we live in a Metro market, where there are 3 million people in a 45-minute radius of where we live. The city we work in is 9 square miles and has 18,000 people.

Finding 75-100 lawn accounts is a minor deal. Naturally, you may have to expand your route as you get more rural or countryside. If you live in a primary metro / suburban market or even have a sprawling section of town, you may have a pocket of customers and another grouping 15 minutes away. That's okay! You can always create your mow routes based on being in a particular subdivision on one day and a different neighborhood on another day.

Similarly, you can be on the North side of town one day, the East side of the city two other days, the South side of town your last two days, and so on. The biggest takeaway for building your routes is establishing service areas, drawing a hardline boundary, and sticking to it! I don't care if your brother-in-law or Aunt Susie lives across the street from your boundary zone, don't do it! To establish route density and "thicken in" your service area, you must have defined boundaries where you provide service!

Fast forward a handful of years. As our business grew and we got into the nicer subdivisions, my goal was to take over and become the dominant lawn care provider. Know what's better than mowing three lawns in a subdivision? Mowing 30 lawns! When we branched into a new subdivision, we had to build our way up. It always started with one customer, one new client that was willing to take us on. That's all we needed! A chance to get our foot in the door, do a good job, and grow from there. Often we would create customer referral programs, giving our current customers two free mows if they referred a neighbor who signed up for weekly service. Other times we became friends with the HOA and asked if they'd be willing to make a community Facebook post sharing about our service. We often found that the clients we picked up were already advocating on our behalf! You want to talk about a fantastic feeling, that is!

One of the questions I get most is: "Brian, can you make good money in lawn care?" My simple answer is always YES! The biggest tip I can share is what we've been talking about in this chapter - insane route density. In the beginning we were all over the place, servicing dozens of subdivisions and areas of town. In one subdivision, we had two lawns, in another we had three, in another, a pocket of five, and so forth. What turned our business around was when we eliminated the outliers and focused on four or five key subdivisions. That changed everything for us. If you're in a major city, focus on one side of town instead of driving all over or having routes on different days around town.

The more often you are in a subdivision the more credibility you have and your brand will exponentially increase. You become the authority when your rig is parked in the same subdivision for 5, 6, and 7 hours a day. Everyone knows of you, and you become "the guy" for that subdivision. This is how you can generate $1,000-$1,500 in daily revenue per crew without even breaking a sweat. There are now times when we unload the mower from the trailer and "hop lawn to lawn," cutting, trimming, and blowing without ever "racking" the mower. The second guy on the team is responsible for driving the rig from home to home, while the guy on the mower is responsible for cutting, blowing, and zipping to the next property. It's beautiful when you can mow a lawn in 15-20 minutes (or less!) and mow 12-15 lawns by lunch! Once you come back and get your second wind for the day, you can easily tackle another 10-15 properties. This strategy has been one of our most important keys to success, no doubt about it. We have examples now in our business where we tackle 35+ lawns, including the 7-acre HOA for that subdivision on certain mow days and can post up to $2000 in revenue by 4:30 pm. It's not that wild to believe!

My heart goes to the folks who fail to recognize that windshield time is the kiss of death for their business year after year. We get paid to rack hours up on our machines, period. He who logs the most hours (at the right price!) wins! It's that simple. It takes time to build great routes and to thicken up your route density, but when you do, it is a beautiful thing. It takes about five years to establish great route density in your area so patience is vital. Continuously market those subdivisions, put out yard signs, talk to the HOA, and take over those parts of town or subdivisions to generate significant revenue.

Chapter Nine

# Gear Up! Building Your Fleet

When I decided to get back into lawn care and take care of the original ten to fifteen clients, I returned to the equipment I had used years before. I had a reliable push mower, a few big box store brand trimmers and blowers, and that was it. When I was a teenager push-mowing lawns in the trailer park, that equipment setup sufficed. It could have been more efficient, but it didn't break the bank either. By the time I had decided to get back into the business, I had begun researching commercial-grade equipment and tried to understand what my company needed to go to the next level. After scouring the internet, watching review videos on YouTube, and picking up catalogs on as many commercial name-brand mowers as possible, I finally decided on the next upgrade. It was a 48" Exmark Viking walk-behind, complete with a hydro-static drive assembly, ECS controls, and a 15hp engine. This mower was the Cadillac of walk-behind mowers back in the day, and the price tag was a cool five thousand dollars. I will be honest; this number scared the you-know-what out of me!

You see, back when this was all forming up, I had just turned 20 years old, and five thousand dollars was a lot of money back then! Just a few years prior, I was purchasing my first car for around ten thousand dollars, and now I am about to buy a lawn mower for five grand. Are you kidding? My understanding of finances, credit, and cash flow back then was so minimal it's hard even to paint an accurate picture. I might have been looking at something that cost one hundred thousand dollars because that's what it felt like at the time. Was I in over my head? I thought so the day I signed and financed that new mower.

I knew it was the right choice, but I am telling you what, I was officially back in the lawn business when I signed on that dotted line if you know what I mean. Realistically, what other skin in the game did I have before then? I had some lawn flyers made up, purchased a few shirts with my company name on them, and that was it! Now I was on the hook for 36 monthly payments for this lawn mower, and if I didn't put it to work, it might as well have been a fancy red paperweight!

That mower was a staple part of our business for the first four years, where we logged an estimated 1,000+ hours on that machine. I purchased a sulky (a rear platform you stand on attached to the mower) for that unit and replaced the bearings and wheels a few times before we finally got rid of that machine. Over the years, our equipment arsenal has grown from zero-turn mowers to stand-on and everything in between. That Exmark Viking walk-behind mower still holds a special place in my memories because it was the mower that started it all. I still remember how nervous I was signing on for that mower back in the day, but I'm so glad I did. That was when Brian's Lawn Maintenance became a real business.

When choosing the right lawn mower, one needs to address a handful of variables to ensure that you pick the suitable unit for your fleet. I've seen it broken down into three equipment setups that are the most popular for a lawn care professional. It goes simply like this: Setup number one includes larger zero-turn mowers for wide open properties. Setup number two includes medium-sized zero-turn mowers and a stand-on or walk-behind mower for smaller parcels and those with gated backyards. Setup number three usually consists of one or two stand-on or walk-behind mowers that are 32-48" in size that are perfect for smaller lawns such as urban properties or those areas that have gated back yards. As you build your fleet, choosing the right brand becomes less important than choosing the right size of mower for your properties.

All name brands are making great mowers that make tall grass short these days. I wouldn't get lost in sticking with a particular mower as much as I would be concerned with partnering up with a great local equipment dealer. What mower brand you start with has little to do with the up-time you can deliver by having a quality service department to take care of your purchase after the sale. A quick tip: stick with the mower brand closest to you that your local equipment dealer sells. Service after the sale is going to be incredibly important. Downtime is a killer in our business, so you have to stick with a brand that A: makes a great product and B: can be serviced on time and close to home. You may prefer one brand but consider this: pick a brand close to you and build a relationship with that local dealer. They are the backbone and your secret weapon to keep everything moving.

As your clientele grows, you can always add a stand-on mower or a gated backyard mower to your setup. But if nothing else, get a quality zero-turn mower that can be your work mule and help you to get as many lawns done as possible in a day. A quick tip: commercial zero-turn mowers are in a league of their own compared to residential units! Stay away from the big box stores and residential entry equipment for homeowners. These units will not stand up to the daily wear and tear and abuse you put them through. I promise you, spend a few extra bucks if needed and get the best equipment you can afford - you'll be so glad you did.

Let's talk briefly about hand tools i.e., trimmers, blowers, and edgers. The best suggestion I can make for these are, firstly, invest in what you need and, secondly, grow your fleet as your needs increase. Only buy three or four of each unit once you need them. Grow this part of your fleet on a shoestring budget. I'd get one of each handheld tool and build your fleet over time. Trust me, hand tools will make or break your efficiency, almost more than your workhorse mower. Budget a reasonable $1,000-$1,500 for this area of your business! Buy the best units you can at the time and stretch to get the higher-end model if you can; you'll be so glad you did. The extra equipment like chainsaws, hedge trimmers, and combi-tools can be added in years two and three, but now, let's stick with the basics. Quicktip: stick to a good quality 2-stroke oil and pay attention to your mix ratios! These higher-end pieces of equipment need to operate effectively for peak performance! Don't cheap out on gas station oil packs and cheap repair parts. Please keep them in tip-top shape and go with that brand's 2-stroke oil.

I am wrapping up this chapter with one final thought on financing equipment. Some folks like to leverage the debt (usually 0% interest) on gear, and some love keeping their business debt free. Either way works for me, as long as you're growing the top-line and bottom-line numbers. It is a delicate balance between using OPM (other people's money) and using your own. I suggest you to keep your cash and finance equipment at 0% if you can get it. Keep your cash as a reserve or use it to fund labor, materials, and marketing, which can help you grow your business exponentially. Once you have multiples in the bank of what you owe on a piece of equipment, then and only then should you consider getting rid of that zero percent interest loan. I'm open to folks running their business debt-free, but leverage what you can and get your business to the altitude as quickly as possible. You'll need cash to do it, so weigh the options carefully as you decide to get your business started and as your business continues to grow.

# Chapter Ten

# The Most Overlooked Item By Far

When I started my business, I pushed my lawn mower around from house to house, never really thinking about how I needed to transport my equipment. When I started, I often threw my setup in the back of my car to shuttle it from client to client. It could have been a more professional-looking setup, but it worked! Add a few bungee cords to keep the trunk lid down, and no one was the wiser that I had a mower stuffed back there! Of course, I felt a little embarrassed every time I took the mower out but I didn't know any better, and frankly, I didn't care. No one would make me feel inadequate about my business or lawn care setup. I was on a mission, remember?!

One thing I didn't consider, though. Now that I was spreading my wings and getting calls for work in subdivisions 10 minutes down the road, I suddenly incurred an issue that I didn't have before. How the heck was I going to get this equipment across town safely? Driving it a few minutes down the road in the same sub-division is one thing, but transporting a mower half-sticking out of my trunk didn't seem safe nor scream the professional image I was trying to project. I needed a solution, and I needed one fast.

Remember, I had recently come off unemployment after being fired from my pizza job before that. Now I was working for a fertilizer company making $11 an hour. I didn't have ten grand lying around to cash flow this puppy, no way at all. After a quick Google Search and realizing I had to transport this new 48" Exmark mower, I settled on a 5'x8' utility trailer from Tractor Supply. Back in the day, these trailers were the swiss army knives of trailers. People used them to transport their ATVs, move firewood, or transport a garden tractor to their vacant property or up north cabin to mow the grass a few times a year. For only $800 out the door, it wasn't a bad proposition either!

Thankfully I was able to pay for this utility trailer in cash, and after a bit of back and forth with my brother's Dodge Durango, we successfully trailered it home. Brian, did you say Dodge Durango? We'll get to that in a minute; hang tight. Not everyone starts with a mack daddy truck and trailer setup as you might imagine! I had to work my way up! That little utility trailer was perfect for what I needed in those early years of my business. We added simple trailer racks for the gas cans, trimmers, and blowers, and our weekend warrior setup was fully displayed. We might've been the new guy on the block, but you would've thought with how I took care of that setup that I felt like I was Brightview (They're a billion-dollar green industry business!)!

For the most part, trailers will come in two variations that you'll need on the regular: a utility trailer (or open trailer) and an enclosed trailer. Utility or open-style trailers are precisely that, a trailer with open decking with side rails that are great for transporting equipment. They come in various sizes and configurations of almost any type these days. The most common are 4'x8', 6'x'10', 6'x14', 7'x14', and 7'x18'. A couple upsides: they are great for lawnmowers and landscaping equipment as they are air-cooled and can provide easy access to your equipment by simply reaching over and accessing them as you pull up curbside to mow a property. There are downsides, however: ease of theft, open to the elements (rain/sun fade), and items can dislodge or even fall off! It's never a good day when you get to a property and realize you're missing a gas can, string trimmer, or God-Forbid a backpack blower, whether from potholes, train tracks, or the thief that snatches something as you run in a store quickly or while filling up your equipment at the gas station. Trust me, we've all been there, and it stinks! Make sure you lock up your equipment whenever possible with these styles of trailers because people are always watching!

Next up, enclosed trailers! One of my favorite types of trailers to use for so many reasons which we'll list here. Number one: they're a rolling billboard for your business! It's more challenging to put signage on your utility trailer but an enclosed trailer can be a massive advertisement for your business as it rolls through town! Number two: equipment safety and security. Once you're done at the end of the day and have the trailer dropped off, lock it up and have the peace of mind that your equipment is secured! No more unloading and loading every night and morning. Your equipment is dry, out of the elements reducing unnecessary wear from the sun and ready to go. I know guys who prefer enclosed trailers because it's their mobile command center with some even installing solar panels, AC units, microwaves, and folding tables for crew lunches.

In the beginning, you may roll with a utility trailer and decide to upgrade to an enclosed trailer; that's typically the evolution I see for most business owners. That was my story! We had to get the funds together for a down payment and the cash flow and client base to support that new purchase. It took us a while to be able to invest in an enclosed trailer, but I am so glad we did. It was one of the best investments we could've made for our business and honestly, I wish I had done it sooner. However, all of this will come at a premium as you can imagine. Be prepared to pay at least five thousand to ten thousand for a quality enclosed trailer compared to a third of that for an open utility-style trailer.

Interest rates and financing for trailers could be better, so if you can't pay cash, at least try to pay them off within a year or less. Equipment trailers are a highly forgiving part of the industry and keep their value well. You can trade or sell your trailer for what you paid if you keep it in decent shape. A quick tip: always get more trailers than you need, within reason. For an open trailer, if you're thinking about a 6'x10' for your zero-turn lawn mower, go 7'x14' so you can store two units. Are you thinking about going 7'x14' for an enclosed trailer? Consider going 7'x16' or 8.5'x16' so you can store two units! You'll typically want something 14-16+ feet long for two mowers and seven to eight feet wide for a zero-turn mower, especially if you add a leaf vacuum one day.

Here's my quick rant about trailers that I wish more people would understand: don't cheap out on your equipment trailers! People often overlook spending money on a good trailer which is ridiculous considering that your entire business is riding on it (literally!)! So many times, I see thirty and forty thousand dollars worth of equipment being pulled around on a two thousand dollar trailer with bent axles and four mismatched tires. I've seen them, you've seen them, no doubt. It's insane to me that people will drive down the road in an unsafe fashion, overloading these trailers without any thought about what's riding on them.

Strap your equipment down, keep up on your equipment maintenance, and operate safely. You don't need to break down on the side of the road with a broken leaf spring, a bad bearing, or be pulled over for faulty trailer lighting because you cheaped out on a few hundred bucks to save some money. There are better areas to skimp, but this isn't one! Buy the best trailers you can afford at the time, and keep them operating in tip-top shape.

There's so much riding on your trailers - pay attention to this area of your equipment setup.

If you'd like to learn more about lawn equipment setups and the best features to look for in trailers, I invite you to check out Episodes 152 and 153 of the Fullerton Unfiltered podcast. I did a deep dive for an hour about both topics which will save you a ton of research and homework! When spending big money on these two areas of your business, getting as much knowledge as possible is essential. Do your homework! These are items you want to avoid making a big, costly mistake on!

# Chapter Eleven

# Selecting The Right Truck

One of the questions I receive the most is: "Brian, what is the best work truck to buy?". As you can imagine, that's a complicated answer, but I'll do my best to simplify the topic. Everybody's needs will differ, so let's discuss a few options. I'll first share my story to lay the groundwork.

An interesting set of circumstances allowed me to use my brother's Dodge Durango as my first actual work vehicle. He was off to college at Michigan State University, and as incoming first-and second-year students, they couldn't have cars at the dorms. That meant his Durango was stuck at our place for the summer, which I immediately attempted to commandeer. I was as diplomatic as possible. It was my brother's vehicle but I needed to pull that new trailer around, and this was the best I had access to. I remember my first lawn care setup being hauled around with this vehicle in 2007 and 2008 when gas peaked at $4.50 a gallon! I almost went out of business my first 18 months just due to the rise in gas prices! That Dodge Durango sucked fuel down and to top it off, the fuel gauge was broken and you couldn't even tell how much you had left! The running joke was to stop daily at the gas station before we started and to add $20 to the tank because you never knew where you were at. It's a miracle that we didn't break down on the side of the road because, in those early days,

I barely had twenty dollars extra to put in the tank. Every dime we had was going back into equipment and marketing!

Knowing we needed to upgrade and my brother would soon return from college, I had to get a work truck. Here is a funny story about that red F-150 to prove that you don't need all of your ducks in a row to get things moving. I purchased that truck on a lunch break one day when I worked at the fertilizer company, sight unseen! During the weeks before, I had been scouring the Internet trying to find the best truck and found this one for sale at a dealer near my fertilizer route! I thought I couldn't make it to that side of town in the evening as it was too far of a drive. But I could take an extended lunch break, sign on the dotted line, grab the keys, and come back later after business hours to drive the truck home, and that's precisely what I did!

I remember it like it was yesterday when I picked up that first work truck. This truck was one of my finest achievements at the time because the vehicle symbolized everything about my new business. That walk-behind mower I mentioned earlier made me feel like I had a real business but that new red pickup truck outwardly let people know we meant business! It was my char- iot, and I felt like we were in high cotton when I picked it up. Call me old fashioned, but there's something about your first truck and the mobile business card that it can feel like for your new enterprise. It wasn't the fanciest truck; it didn't have all the bells and whistles, nor was it a three-quarter ton or above, but it was precisely what we needed at the time. Over the years, we dreamed about upgrading to larger trucks, but in the beginning, you just need to get moving.

That F-150 was the biggest blessing I could've asked for in the early stages of my business. For the next several years, it was a reliable workhorse that did the trick, hauling our equipment around and helping us to get established. I ended up selling that truck a few years back, but I sometimes wish I hadn't. We outgrew its capabilities, but it would've been fun to hold onto it just for a keepsake. You always remember your first truck as corny as it sounds, but it meant the world to me. If you know, you know.

Let's now get into quality metrics and what you're ideally looking for in your first truck. Number one, you want something reliable. We can get into the nitty-gritty of a half-ton, three-quarter ton, four-by-two, four-by-four, Ford, Chevy, and Ram, but the number one factor in shopping for is reliability. I say that because we must make it to the job site, complete our work, and return safely. I don't care how fancy your truck is or how rusted out it is as long as it allows you to get your work done.

We'd all like a fancier truck, something new that is still intact aesthetically, but finding a mechanically sound truck is more important than leather seats or fancy technology. A work vehicle with less than 100,000 miles is a great place to start. Although not as fancy, older vehicles can offer many benefits such as a greater ease of mechanical repairability instead of needing a computer to fix or diagnose something wrong. Today's trucks provide a bevy of technology, but most require a laptop to work on, not a set of wrenches! To start, consider investing in a gently used truck with low mileage and minimal wear on the exterior paint. Sometimes it can be like finding a needle in a haystack, but stick with it; these diamonds in the rough are worth the hunt! Then once your cash flow increases, consider upgrading.

A few other items of mention are engine options, four-wheel drive, and half-ton vs. three-quarter ton. Let's cover those for a quick minute. The age-old question of gas vs. diesel will be debated and contested until the end of time. Here is my opinion: go with a gas-powered engine unless you're hauling a heavy load daily. Think skid steers, dump trailers, mini excavators, etc. That's where I suggest having a diesel for a daily driver. For everyone else, a gas motor is acceptable, including those who plan to plow snow! We've run with gas-powered trucks for a long time and have never had any significant issues with these engines regarding power or reliability.

Another upside is that they're much simpler to work on, and almost any local dealer or mom-and-pop shop can help get you back on the road if you break down. I love diesel engines just as much as the next guy until you get that first repair bill for your engine that costs you three to five thousand dollars. Those are repairs you cannot afford to factor into your first few years in business. If you want, upgrade to diesel trucks after a few years once your company is more robust and your cash flow is better. I recommend getting a four-by-four equipped vehicle for those in a cold weather climate and seeing snow regularly. You'll need it if you decide to plow snow! Warning: please take advantage of this area of your truck if you plan to get into snow removal because a four-by-two truck will not cut it, no matter what your brother-in-law says! Unless you live anywhere below the Midwest rust belt and don't regularly see snow, I would roll with a four-by-two vehicle. Lastly, most of us will start with a half-ton truck, whether it's your truck or one you purchase for the business. Those will work just fine initially, but over time you'll want to expand and upgrade to a three-quarter ton or one-ton. The suspensions, chassis, and capabilities of these trucks will be necessary as your workload and demands increase for your vehicles.

A quick tip: a clean vehicle is the best way to make a positive first impression! Take pride in your truck, and keep it as clean as possible! Even if the truck is a little bit older and has some surface rust, don't let that be an excuse for not keeping the exterior and interior clean! Our trucks are often the front-line impression we make on our customers and prospective clients, so keep them clean! Five dollars goes a long way at the coin wash and vacuums when stopping at the local car wash once a week (or more often if needs dictate). Take pride in your vehicles, wash them down, add some tire shine, and make it part of a routine to keep them clean. Riding down dirt roads and mud-bogging with your truck is fun in your teens and twenties, but you're a business owner now. Keep a respectable image personally and professionally, as they are an extension of you and your brand. The time will come when you can reinvest in better work vehicles and purchase extra equipment like dump trucks, box trucks, and cab-overs. In the beginning, get yourself a reliable work truck that can be used as your primary workhorse that will go the distance.

Chapter Twelve

# Organizing The Back Of The House

So far in this book, we've spent considerable time on what I call the front of the house - the topics that usually get the most time and consideration. I have to be honest though. After a handful of years in business, our company was on life support. We were hanging on by a thread because I hadn't given any serious time or attention to our books and office work. In contrast, we were great at doing the physical work in the business but my mentality about running a real business needed improvement. I should have paid more serious attention to how we ran the company, our financials, and if we were creating significant profit. We were spinning our tires in the mud, and it showed. I was ashamed of how brittle our company was and the lack of financial literacy I had, and I was flat-out embarrassed about our operation.

I know the following topics may not be as sexy a conversation as equipment and vehicle purchases, but make no mistake, they're equally (if not more!) necessary to have a successful company. Many of you have heard the acronym KISS, which stands for "Keep It Simple Silly". I plan to do that in the following few chapters as we discuss how to take your passion (lawn & landscaping) into a business you can be proud of. I promise to make the following few chapters simple to understand because I want to see you succeed at the highest level with your new company. One thing that amazes me is how many people make such a simple business model and industry so challenging. It doesn't have to be that way.

One of the biggest heartaches I have, and why this topic has become so passionate for me, is hearing all of the failure stories of people in the green industry and how they never made any real money. I often listen to folks passionate about their work, but they spend their time on things other than running their business like a real business. After all, mowing grass and slinging mulch is way more fun than invoicing customers, collecting payments, and monitoring the financial health of your business, am I right? It amazes me how many people would rather chase the next landscaping job or rush to mow the following property without spending any recent time or activity in the office keeping tabs on their business. What is the point of running to the next job site if you never collected payment or did an autopsy to see if you made a healthy profit? I see it all too often, and I want to ensure that you never get into the habit of a rat in a wheel chasing the next job and never taking the time to understand that you're building a real business, not just owning a job.

My first recommendation is to get yourself linked with a CRM to help you keep track of and manage your business. A CRM (or Customer Relationship Manager) is software designed explicitly for our industry and is what you need from day one to keep track of your customers and workflow. Every business has a customer information database, and lawn care should be the same. There are a couple of great CRMs out there, but the one we've found works the best for us is a platform called Yardbook. It's the iPhone version of lawn care software: it's simple to use, easy to navigate, and it's completely free. In this CRM, you can add all your customer information when they sign up for service and add notes about the customer's property, lot size, address, and so much more. You can use a CRM to send invoices, collect payments, and approve estimates. Gone are the days of carbon copy invoices, sending out physical quotes, or collecting checks in the mail (more on that in a second!).

With the increased technology use in our industry, we've seen many new options to help you manage your business. Whichever CRM you choose, please do your best to stick with it as you build your empire. Jumping ship from one platform to another can be extremely daunting as your business grows, so do your due diligence now. Request a demo, and make sure you pick a CRM related to the services you plan to offer. A quick tip: some services are free, and others require a monthly subscription. Just because something is free, that doesn't make it great. Similarly, just because something costs a small monthly car payment to help you run your business doesn't indicate it's excellent, either. You have to find the right CRM for you.

Having a good CRM is good - how you use it is where it makes all the difference. Take the time to learn the platform you sign up with, and I promise, the technology will help you streamline your operation but it only works if you use it. Don't get caught up with industry trends, fancy widgets, or features that look shiny on the outside but do little to help you practically manage your business. I often see folks distracted by "shiny object syndrome." Some flashy exclusive feature that no one else has that promises to make all of your problems go away! Remember, shiny bait doesn't only work with fish! You want to avoid getting caught trying something new with a striking feature and pay attention to the fact that the software needs to be more encompassing to help you run your business effectively.

Managing your lawn care business with a CRM is a vital tool in your lawn care business success, so it keeps track of your customers and day-to-day business activities. Excellent accounting software like Quickbooks is paramount to give you the needed one-two punch for managing your business growth. Accounting software and CRMs are entirely different; accounting software does not replace a good CRM, and vice versa. They are completely different in what they track and manage in your business. We'll talk more about having a bookkeeper in a future chapter, but keep it in your mind to register with a quality CRM and bookkeeping software like Quickbooks.

Before we rush out the door, there's one last area we need to address, and that is the topic of insurance. There are a few primary forms of insurance that you'll need when you establish your business. The two central policies you'll need are General Liability and Commercial Auto. General Liability is there for accidental damages you cause due to your equipment, and Commercial Auto is there to insure your vehicle during business use. These are two areas you want to make sure to take advantage of! Shop these policies often, but ensure insurance coverage for the sites you manage. A good rule of thumb at the beginning for General Liability is One Million Dollars in coverage. This amount will satisfy the insurance requirements for most commercial businesses and give you the peace of mind you need when operating your equipment.

While we are on insurance, I recommend a few other policies to keep in mind. There's a running joke that says: "never ask your insurance agent if you need more insurance!". While I always get a kick out of that line, it's true. Don't let that deter you from carefully considering the following policies to give you additional peace of mind and coverage for you and your business: Short-Term and Long-Term Disability, Inland Marine policies which cover your mowers and more extensive equipment, Trailer Insurance, Life Insurance, a general Tool Floater policy (to insure hand tools),

Health Insurance, and of course, Workers' Comp. These additional policies cost a pretty penny, so make sure you shop them annually during the off-season to get the best rates possible.

A quick tip: when comparing policies from different agencies, always ensure the policies are viewed as apples-to-apples and keep an eye on the deductibles. Some agents may be able to beat the price on your current policy but comb through it to make sure they didn't play any tricks, including messing with your deductible or total coverage. Oh, and keep an eye out for additional add-ons you don't need. One item that rings a bell is terrorism insurance. If you don't need it, remove it. Remember this; only some insurance companies can get you the best rate when comparing apples to apples. Some insurance companies specialize in certain types of insurance coverage and others are not competitive, no matter how hard your agent tries. There's something to be said about loyalty. Still, you need to run a profitable business, and insurance can be a heavy line item on your P&L. Shop it often, compare quotes, and make sure you have the adequate coverage you need for every step of your business growth.

I want to make sure you're taking insurance coverage seriously. You do not want to be out of business due to a wreck or accident longer than you need. Insurance is not an area to fib on or have gray areas with your insurance agent. Be honest, and include them in the conversation about what you're doing with your business. Any time we evaluate a new purchase, from equipment to a new vehicle, we are preemptively on the phone with our insurance agent to shop rates to factor in that additional overhead. Insurance is an absolute necessity - I'd like to think an uninsured business might as well be no business at all! I've seen too many horror stories of people not getting General Liability Insurance, Commercial Auto, or Disability Income, only to have a freak situation that laid them up for several weeks or months.

Please carefully consider adding these policies to your business as soon as possible; the peace of mind they offer is second to none. Accidents do happen, and they occur in the unlikeliest of scenarios. Make sure you have adequate coverage and are prepared for anything because one day it just may happen. And instead of that event derailing your business, it will be a small road bump.

## Chapter Thirteen

# Building Your Team

As your company grows, you'll quickly realize that you won't be able to do it all on your own; at least, that was my experience. Unfortunately, I only figured this out long after I was in business. We did our best to navigate the different hats we were wearing as business owners but they never received the time and attention they deserved. It's hard to juggle being out in the field producing work and working "on" the business behind the scenes. I've noticed one side usually suffers when you're an owner-operator style of business so, naturally, you need to hire help.

One of my friends named Tom says "Business is a team sport and the three most dangerous words in business are 'Do It Yourself'." From day one you may only need some of these folks as part of your team, but remember this chapter as your business grows. Whether you plan to build a solo owner-operator size business or the next regional business doing ten million, you will need help. There's the holy trinity: a bookkeeper, payroll provider, and certified public accountant (CPA). When it comes to helping your business stay organized, be industry-compliant, manage your financials, and navigate your taxes, these are the three horsemen to help you do battle.

Let's start with the most glaring question regarding running a business - how to manage and handle your bookkeeping. A bookkeeper helps track your receipts, correctly log expenses and write-offs, and ensure regular reporting about your business's financial strength. Examples of monthly reporting can include your P&L (profit and loss), cash flow analysis, and balance sheet, to name a few. Having someone help you professionally manage your books is essential. If I could share any one tip to recommend from day one, it would be this: stay away from the dreaded shoebox full of receipts.

The mad dash to get your books in order during tax time can be a nightmare, especially once your business grows north of $100k in revenue. The most heartache and confusion I've ever experienced came from not having my books in order. It doesn't have to be that way! Hire a competent bookkeeper, register with an accounting program like Quickbooks, and let them help you navigate organizing and completing proper record keeping for your business. You'll be so glad you did because there's nothing better than laying your head down on your pillow at night knowing that your books are in order, your money is yours, and everything is organized correctly. Trust me on that one!

The next team member you should consider adding very quickly is a payroll service to help navigate employee hires and subcontractors. As your business grows, hiring help is incredibly important as you aim to hit higher revenue production in your company. The days of paying your friends via cash, PayPal, and Venmo should be a thing of the past. I'm not saying you can't have a buddy help once in a while to help you shore things up on a busy day, but be forewarned; you're skating on thin ice if they're helping you regularly and you're still paying them cash. Paying people under the table will catch up with you! Don't shortcut the shortcut, do things correctly and add your team members to your payroll. Hiring a payroll service doesn't have to be a daunting task, either. It's easier and more manageable than you may believe.

Simply put, a payroll service helps to navigate both state and federal tax withholding, issues paychecks to your team members and helps you stay compliant with payroll taxes and correct filing of forms for tax time. A quick example of this would be: you pay someone on your team $20 an hour, and they worked 40 hours this week, totaling $800. You will report those hours bi-weekly on a weekday to your payroll company, giving them the total hours for the last two periods. That Thursday, funds are usually deducted from your business account, and the correct taxes are withheld for you and your team members. When your banks open on Friday morning around 8 or 9 a.m., your employees will see their paychecks directly deposited into their accounts.

A quick tip: your employees may see a difference between their hourly rate and hours worked compared to what is deposited into their account! This gap is the difference between "gross" and "net." In this example, where your employee worked 80 hours in two weeks at $20 an hour, their gross check would have been $1,600 but it was only $1,350, for example. That's the withholding that your payroll provider helps collect and sends those funds to the various state and federal organizations for payroll taxes. Sometimes you need to coach younger new hires on this process because it can be confusing that not everything they earn, they keep!

When searching for a quality payroll service provider you can look at a small-town provider or a national company. The biggest things to look for are: What are their fees per paycheck issued? Do they offer weekly or biweekly payroll (we do bi-weekly)? And when do they need hours due for the last period? Some have smart apps where you can record hours, other times, you're simply emailing your gal the hours for the previous two weeks. That's it! Super simple.

A quick tip: 1099 subcontractors are very different from W-2 employees. Please make sure you're paying people correctly as they join your team! If someone is coming on staff and utilizing your equipment, trucks, mowers, and headed to job sites on your determined schedule, this qualifies them as a W-2 employee. Hiring someone to perform a specific task with their equipment on their schedule allows them as a 1099 subcontractor. Your payroll can help you to have correct forms filled out and collected, including a W-9 for 1099s and a W-4 for employees. Warning! Do not 1099 friends or family that help you semi-regularly and pay them as a subcontractor; this can catch up with you and cost you a significant payroll tax burden in the future. You need to add them to your payroll, even if they only work with you a few hours a week or on a part-time basis. It always pays to do things correctly, and the last thing you need is the State Department coming down on you for back payroll taxes.

The last member in the trinity of your team is a Certified Public Accountant or CPA for short. I will tell you this, the person who will make the most significant difference on your team when helping you will be your CPA. Remember, the role of a CPA is to help you file your taxes and structure your business to help you reduce your tax bill legally. Quarterly conversations about navigating your income and expenses, how you're structuring your write-offs, and where your cash flow is at are meaningful conversations you should have with your CPA. I know that hiring a CPA can start with hundreds of dollars and quickly escalate to thousands to help you with your taxes, but I promise you, it is money well spent! A quality professional should save you or make you more than what it costs to invest in their services, and a CPA should be no different.

I've heard hundreds of horror stories of unorganized, passive, laissez-faire CPAs who wanted to file your return and collect their fee. There needs to be a partnership, a conversation about your goals, and a strategy for approaching your tax return. I wish there was a silver bullet on this one, but you will have to navigate and hire a quality CPA that you trust and believe will help you as a critical team member with your new enterprise. Taxes are one of the topics I get incredibly passionate about because it's your money! Not the government's!

I promise you the more you earn the more you start paying attention to your business affairs, and taxes are part of this conversation! Taxes are automatically withheld from your paycheck when you're an employee, but that's not the case as a business owner! When you're self-employed, you "pay in," not the other way around! When you collect revenue, you owe taxes on that income! Of course, write-offs and deductions help reduce that tax bill, but you will most likely pay quarterly for estimated taxes on the revenue you generate. You must set a portion of that aside for your tax liability at the end of each year. Until you have a CPA helping you navigate these conversations and projections, keep 15-20% of your gross revenue aside for your quarterly taxes.

A quick tip: honesty is always the best policy, even more so with your CPA! It would be best if you had the most honest conversations possible with two people in your life: your spouse and your CPA. Your CPA is essential to your company and your financial success! Refrain from skirting around issues or fibbing when discussing expenses, purchases, or future investments in your business. They will help you maximize your results and sometimes talk you back to reality when needed! My conversations with my CPA have helped increase my financial IQ tenfold and given me the courage and wisdom I need to navigate my personal and business finances. If you want to grow your company and use this business to build wealth, please consider hiring a quality CPA. It will be some of the best money you've ever spent.

Let's wrap this chapter up by answering one question I often receive when relating to bookkeepers, payroll providers, and hiring a CPA: who do you look for, and what makes a good team member? Great question! Here are three litmuses I have for building your team for every person you bring on. Number one, do you have chemistry? Having someone you can create a friendship with that doesn't look down on you and wants to help you grow is incredibly important. If you don't "hit it off" with those people, they may not be a good fit for you.

Number two: a teacher's heart. Find someone who cannot only solve your problems but helps you understand the "why" of what you're doing that day and not just the "how." Of course, you're hiring them to complete a specific task but there must also be an excitement to share and include you in the decision making and conversation. I recommend avoiding someone who fast-talks around you or glosses over topics. You want to understand the process even if they provide the correct answers. A non-receptive team member, or someone who doesn't educate you along the way, could be a potential red flag to consider replacing them on your team.

Number three: they are competent at their job/service/task. Competency may be harder to assess as you start a business because you are still learning the terminology, but constantly evaluate your team members and ensure they are as effective as possible. It's not your team members' role to solve your problems, necessarily. They are here to help you navigate your goals and guide you as an advisor. When you come to a meeting, be prepared with a list of questions. They can make suggestions and offer a sounding board for your game plan, but the motivation to do that starts with you. As your knowledge increases about these topics, you're able to better work with your advisors. Don't be afraid to check their work, poke around, and ask questions.

I hate to say it, but I had a CPA for almost a decade that I later found utterly incompetent! I had the wrong person on my team, and after a handful of conversations towards the tail end of our relationship, I realized we were on a different wavelength. He was focused on W-2s and simple 401K-type tax returns. I was a business owner with multiple entities, income streams, and unique investment strategies. We weren't a good fit for each other, so we ended our working relationship. Remember, you can draft new members of your team at any time. Competency is the ante, but continuous professional development and education should also be a prerequisite for both sides! Find someone still learning and growing and coming to you with ideas to help your business grow, not just the other way around.

Chapter Fourteen

# Where The Rubber Meets The Road

Iknow we've spent a lot of time getting ready, but now we are finally ready to hit the road and start cutting lawns! Remember, a rocket can use 80% of its energy to get into space! Starting a business can be no different. I want you to have the correct foundation as you grow and how not to step on any potential land mines with your business. You can't build a skyscraper on the same foundation that you would a ranch home, and going back to excavate is a daunting task - trust me, I know. I, unfortunately, built my business the opposite way growing for years and realizing that we had to go back and fix a bunch of areas. I promise you, it wasn't fun! So before we rush out the door to start tackling lawn and landscaping jobs, ensure you have your t's crossed and your i's dotted in the preceding chapters. Now, can we get to the fun stuff?!

Let's talk about your first-week mowing lawns and what you can expect because anything that can happen will happen, as you know! I remember my first week of getting back into lawn care with my new commercial equipment and on the first lawn, I went to engage the blades on my lawn mower, the spindle fell out, and I dropped my lawn mower blade on the pavement. I'm not even kidding. I was in utter disbelief and shock. Thank God nothing happened that could've damaged the mower, pulleys, or other blades! I wasn't ready for that one, as you can imagine! I laughed and thought this is my illustrious return to cutting lawns! I sometimes wonder if the neighbors or the client were looking out the window, wondering why I was wrenching on my new lawn mower right on their front lawn! I've had to swallow my pride and ego more times than I remember with this business, and you know what? It didn't kill me! This event should have been an omen from day one, ha!

My first experience when mowing lawns that week was one of excitement and nervousness. We didn't have an overwhelming schedule (not yet!), so it was an easy-does-it pace for the first few lawns. I wanted to get the hang of the lawn mower, the controls, and how it worked. The weekend before, I had taken my rig to a Target parking lot to practice around cones, but this was the real deal! One wrong move or mistake could cost me hundreds in costly repairs for both me and the client. The first cut went pretty smooth after I reattached the blade and spindle. I trimmed and blew off the clippings, and we were on our way to the next lawn.

If you've never mowed lawns commercially, I invite you to watch and learn how the pros do it before cutting your first blade of grass. Watch some great videos on YouTube of folks mowing lawns so you can see how they do it. Another great resource is our training course called "How To Professionally Cut Grass" on our training website. Believe it or not, it is one of our most downloaded and watched resources! There we spell out exactly, in real-time, how to edge, mow, trim and blow a residential property. Cutting your lawn is different from mowing a lawn for hire. There's a process to it and efficiency is everything. Remember, we're on the clock, and time is money. As simple as mowing a lawn can be, there's still a rhyme and a reason why we do what we do.

My suggestion on your first day as you start your new business is this: take it slow! Try to mow a handful of properties on your first day, not ten or twenty. Aim for five or six. Give yourself the margin to do a good job and to learn your equipment. Speed comes from familiarity, but in the beginning, let's aim for quality. In a week or two, you'll be able to ramp up your production and mow ten or twenty lawns a day, but take your time before you load up your days in the beginning. The biggest thing to remember when building your routes and starting your business is this: it's a marathon, not a sprint! There will be endless lawns to mow for the rest of your career, but let's learn how to correctly take care of our new properties first and work on ramping up our production second.

When it comes to adding to your route and scheduling your days, I have a few suggestions. Number one: load your days from Monday to Friday, not Friday to Monday. Here's why: everybody and their brother wants to have their lawn mowed on Friday, and although you can accommodate a few, you can only do it for some. Also, you're instantly stuck working Saturday if there's any rain on Thursday or Friday. Hey, I love working Saturdays just as much as the next guy, but I like to do it because it's a choice and not because I have to.

When customers ask for a specific day, please listen carefully and do what makes sense for your route, not what works best for them. You cannot run a business that caters exclusively to their preferred mow day; it will drive you crazy. Instead, as discussed in our chapter on route density, build your customer base in specific areas and parts of town and schedule those days accordingly. We front-load all of our commercial work on Mondays and Tues-days when commercial and industrial clients expect their lawns to look their best for the week. We cut most of our residential on Wednesday and Thursday to have their properties looking manicured for the weekend. Friday is a makeup day for us and an extra day for landscaping or auxiliary services. Long story short, backfill Monday through Friday, and even consider leaving an extra day for makeup on your route due to bad weather.

Let's talk about the weather for a quick second because it's, unfortunately, one of our industry's biggest struggles, no matter which way you cut it. You can have backup plan after backup plan and contingencies galore but eventually, the weather will get the best of you. Rain days, hurricanes, tropical storms, and scorching hot days are problematic conditions we work through in our business. There's no silver bullet to navigating these conditions, and it's challenging no matter what anyone says. Working outdoors is one make-it-or-break-it benchmark for those who stick with the industry long-term compared to those who can't handle it. It can get the best of you and your attitude if you let it.

A friend of mine named Andy said it best. He told the story about working one day outdoors and someone said it must be great working outdoors all the time. He smugly replied: "When was the last time you worked outside when you didn't want to, or the weather wasn't nice?" It is a great revelation to those who decide to work for themselves outdoors when they realize that the elements are only sometimes cooperative! If I only worked on days when it was convenient and a beautiful 75 degrees and sunny, with light puffy clouds and a ten mph breeze, I would need less than two hands to count on! It's different from the reality of working outdoors, at least here in the Midwest from March through November!

One of the reasons why we leave margin in our schedule is because of the weather as we mentioned before. Another is for equipment delays or employee challenges. It's not always going to be sunshine and rainbows, and I want you to know that going into it. There's a saying out there recently: fast, cheap, and good, pick two. My spin on that is: equipment working, employees showing up, and cooperative weather; pick two. That's just the truth when you work in the trades! Consider having margin in your work schedule for situations like these and many more. Some guys opt to work four 10s, with Friday being a makeup day or for overtime and service calls. Other folks enjoy working 6 am to 4 pm regularly, getting the best of the morning and beating the heat; that works too. Whatever gets the job done! One of the big draws of self-employment is having the flexibility to build your schedule, including taking time off. Whatever you decide to do, be consistent, and communicate with your customers when needed.

# Chapter Fifteen

# It's All About Production

We've talked in the last chapter about where the rubber meets the road. Now, let's shift gears and get our business into overdrive. I don't know about you, but I got back in business for the top 5 reasons, just like most of you: money, money, money, money, and yes, money! I was tired of living paycheck to paycheck, I was tired of living on my boss's terms, and I wanted to start having more options in life. That's one reason why a majority of people go into business for themselves! Not necessarily to be hog nasty rich (whatever that means!), but to have a little more breathing room and better financial opportunity.

Look, I will be honest, there are only a few reasons people don't make it in our industry. Would you like those reasons before you set out on this journey? Weather, challenging working conditions, equipment failure, and demanding customers are all real struggles within our industry, no doubt about it - but what I've found to be the truth about why people get out of business and go back to a 9 to 5 is this: they weren't making money. They never cracked the code to having a profitable and successful business they could be proud of. Look, I've been there, I say this from experience. There was a period of time in our company when we weren't making the profit I thought I should be making. It was very frustrating trying to justify to my wife that things weren't going as well as I had hoped, as you can imagine.

Let's crack the code about the two most significant contributing factors to having a profitable lawn and landscaping business. Number one is having great pricing, and number two is simply production; what are you making per man-hour? We could write an entire book on these two topics themselves but let's break down what we mean for each subject so you can understand them better.

Regarding great pricing means pricing jobs so that you are profitable. You have to price jobs to make money, that's it, period. I often see people taking on lawn, landscaping, fertilizing, and snow accounts to keep their guys moving or to "earn the job" to get their foot in the door. I will tell you this, that is a horrible way to approach your business. You should aim to make a significant margin on everything your company does, or why bother? Some folks will discount work or have a loss leader to get new clients; that's hogwash. I'd much rather see folks enjoy time off with their family and hang it up for the day than go on out there and spin their tires with low-cost work that doesn't pay.

If it can be helped, stick with charging premium pricing right out of the gate! It's much easier to get a new client at the right price than to get a customer at a below-average price and try to raise rates in the following seasons. It doesn't work and costs you time, money, and frustration. Trying to become profitable with low-bid customers is like getting water out of a rock! I'm sure there's a way to do it but you'll be out of business before you figure it out. Start from the beginning by charging a fair but premium price. Know what types of margins you are trying to aim for with your business and have your bookkeeper or CPA help you better understand your overhead. Mentorship from professional folks like these will help you to recoup your costs and run a profitable business right out of the gate.

In business, there are going to be hundreds of terms you're going to learn and one of them is "per man-hour rate." You'll see that phrase tossed around once you start going down the rabbit hole of knowing your numbers. A man-hourly rate is simply this: a production rate that you charge for your employees that recovers overhead and creates company profit. You see, in our industry, we are exchanging labor for money. The more labor (production) you turn over, the better. One company with ten employees working 10 hours in the field will generate more revenue than one with one employee. It's a simple math equation. The goal is to create as much production as possible with the highest margins possible. The keys to profitability are great pricing, high production rates, and manageable overhead. Check the pulse of these key performance indicators regularly to navigate your business to success.

The more people you can have produce in the field, the more folks you have recovering your company's overhead. Overhead is anything that you have to pay for which your company needs to exist. That can be a shop, equipment, rent, payroll, insurance, and so much more. You need to recoup these direct costs at a minimum every month to remain in business! As you can imagine, the more people and production hours that you can spread these over, the better! Trying to pay for all of your overhead with only your efforts can be a daunting task, no doubt about it. Having a team of two, three, or four people can help you increase production, recoup overhead, and earn profit for the business. These two items go hand in hand, and they are the backbone of a profitable business! Having a "per man-hour rate" north of $70 is what I would suggest. The industry average is around $55-$60, which I find pretty low, but it gives you a starting point to work off.

Some great calculators can help you price lawns, whether by your hourly rate, man-hour rate, or square footage of the property. The biggest takeaway is this: please don't guess! Just because your lawn buddy who owns a business in town is charging $40 for a weekly mow doesn't mean that is the right price! One of the most concerning elements of our industry is the "What are you getting for a lawn?" question. It's almost irrelevant! Every business is different, including your production rates, overhead, and goals for profitability.

As a rule of thumb, please steer clear of asking peers what they charge. The answers you get will be, at best, embellished and could dramatically affect the future of your business and profitability, and at worst, just plain wrong. The worst thing you can do is ask for help from someone who doesn't know their numbers; the blind leading the blind if you will. Dive into your numbers and ask for help if you need it regarding how to price your lawn and landscaping work. There are plenty of great resources to help you navigate this topic but it requires attention. The days of "$25" lawn cuts should be a thing of the past! P.S. Those numbers were from 1980 anyways; it's been 30 years since those days, and we can do much better!

Tackling your first revenue goal of $100,000 per year is a simple formula you can work backward for. If your man-hour rate is $50 per hour, you need to work 2,000 hours in your business. That can be you working 2,000 hours or having you and a team member both work 1,000 hours each. On average, you'll get around 1,680 working hours out in the field annually due to rainy days and downtime. That means you need to generate almost $60 per man-hour, and so on. Everybody's man-hour rate is and should be different. In Florida, for example, you may be able to work 50 weeks straight, while in the Midwest, you may only get 32 weeks with lawn and landscaping. You may be able to get a premium in higher-end markets and in other markets with low-bid work you may be below average on those numbers. The key is to know how many hours you need to work to recover your overhead and hit profitability in your company.

A quick tip: every individual piece of equipment you own will have its break-even to recoup its cost and generate profit! As you can imagine, production numbers for a zero-turn lawn mower can vary significantly compared to having a landscaping crew running skid steers and laying pavers! One piece of equipment might generate $50 per hour while a hardscape crew might be at $300 per hour or even more! Snow plowing rates can exceed even that! The goal is to know your numbers, and that comes with having a great team to help you navigate and build a game plan for your business. A little time spent on the back end can make all the difference on the front end. Side note: What is the easiest way to know when to turn a customer down? When they start lowballing your rates and involuntarily debating your production rates! Once I have a customer tell me the pricing that they want, (which, more often than not,  doesn't equate to meeting our production rates!), it becomes clear to dismiss that customer as a potential prospect and to say "Next!". I encourage you to do the same!

# Chapter Sixteen

# Getting The Boat
# Close To The Dock

As we near the end of this book, I have to leave you with a personal story that led to us going full-time in our lawn and landscaping business. It's a funny story to tell now, but I promise you 15 years ago that was not the case! I was scared out of my mind because the choice to go full-time in my business wasn't one I necessarily made for myself! I don't know if I ever saw myself going full-time in business for myself, but God had a bigger plan back in 2006. My friend Paul refers to the process of quitting your job and going full-time in business as "getting the boat close to the dock." Before you leap, do your best to get your business and personal affairs in order to make that transition as easy as possible. If getting close to the dock refers to an easy transition, mine was more of a Hail Mary jump as someone pushed me from behind! It wasn't the prettiest, but we made it work! Let me share that story with you quickly because I want to share a few funny lessons from it.

When I was working back at the fertilizer company I decided to get back into lawn care and I had finished the last few months of the season running my business part-time on nights and weekends. I was the glorified weekend warrior, which is why I can relate to folks so well when they're trying to manage a 9 to 5 and grow their business on the side. I did it for a year as I started working for the fertilizer company all through that first season. During the following off-season, we all got laid off and collected unemployment which was customary for this company and its workers.

Every late winter and into early spring, we had a mandatory day back at the local branch for what they effectively called "Spray Training." This was a day dedicated to "getting the rust out" and helping us cover the formalities of returning to full-time employment in the coming weeks once the weather breaks. I still remember this day like yesterday. As I walked into the training classroom, the look on my assistant manager and branch manager's faces was wide-eyed and puzzled. They were shocked to see me roll in which I wasn't picking up on.

We went through the motions that day, performing spray training drills, practicing our truck maneuvering, and filling out any information and forms that had to be updated. As the day was wrapping up, my assistant manager called me over and wanted a quick talk. Sure, I thought, "I wonder what this could be about?" He promptly joked, "I didn't expect to see you today!" with a half chuckle. I had asked, "Why, what's up?". "Well, we thought you had gone full-time with your lawn care business," he said. "No, no, I planned to work here full time and still work the business nights and weekends, just like last year," I said. We had only managed to earn back around 20 regular clients and I was still paying off some of the recently acquired equipment. I was reinvesting every dime and I still needed that steady paycheck!

"Well, that's interesting, you see, because we already filled your truck with somebody else," he said. I laughed because I had been reading self-help books at the time and was working on building a better attitude! I said, "Hey, no big deal, just put me in a different truck! I'm ready to go!". With a long and drawn-out "right" that would make Matthew McCounghey blush, he said, "Brian, I don't think you're picking up on what I'm putting down. You don't work here anymore.". I was stunned! I thought, "Then why didn't you send me home when I got here? Why did I just waste all day doing spray training?!". I was confused, angry, and afraid, all at the same time. A flood of emotions filled my body, and I didn't know what to do. Less than twelve months ago, I had just been laid off at 19 years old, and here I was, not even a year later, having the same talk. The moment I got laid off from the fertilizer company was a significant inflection point. I promised myself, come hell or high water, I would never work for somebody else again.

Feeling defeated, I didn't know what to do next other than pack my belongings and head home. It was late February, and I had about six weeks until the spring rush hit. I had decided right then and there to make a go for it. I would give it everything I had for the next six to eight weeks and move Heaven and Earth to make this a sustainable business that could support me financially. I want to say that this bold proclamation came with a Cinderella ending, but it just wasn't the case. I remember fighting tooth and nail, climbing and crawling my way out of poverty to get this business working. I had no money in savings, no income, and only a few weeks left of unemployment. I was at the lowest of lows.

Knowing I had about six weeks until the season started, I got serious about growing our customer base. I had built an excel budget on my computer and knew precisely how many customers were required to go full-time. I had my annual expenses drawn up, and I knew exactly what I needed to make every month to keep my head above water. It was less than you would think. After all, I was still living at home with my Mom but I was focused on doing anything it took to grow our top-line revenue to solidify going full-time.

I marketed my business so hard those next few weeks, putting out yard signs, calling customers for referrals, and even walking door to door handing out flyers to the more than 4,000 residents in North Wixom. I canvassed the whole town, and you know what? It worked! Within four weeks, we had secured enough customers to double our revenue in business from the previous year, and we were just getting started! When you go all in and go full-time, you can now commit the time you need to grow your revenue and obtain new customers. I often see the hesitancy to go full-time, but you have to trust me when I say once the time is right, you have to make the leap and go for it. You'd be surprised what you can do when you focus on your business fifty to sixty hours a week instead of juggling multiple hats and jobs.

Year two was one of the most challenging periods of the business because with as many breakthroughs as we had from launching our business, we had created new problems as we continued to grow! Perhaps this will be another future book in our series because the stories are endless!

My wife Liz championed a phrase in our relationship - one that we picked up along the way, and that is this: "Make a decision and make it right." So many people ask "When is the best time to go full-time in business?" The honest answer is that it's different for everybody. It's hard to explain the perfect scenario as to when you should go full-time in your business because that answer is unique to your situation. Naturally, you'll want to make sure you have some money in savings, equipment paid down (or off!) as much as possible, and health insurance figured out, to name a few. But the reality is, we didn't have any of those items in place when we jumped, and guess what? It worked out! The reason it worked out is that we made it work. There was no special talent that allowed us to become self-employed. It was pure determination and perseverance.

## Chapter Seventeen

# Begin With The End In Mind

One of the most common questions I was asked during my Highschool Days was this: "What do you want to do when you grow up?" You've heard it, I've heard it. It's the most popular question young adults hear as they near graduation and move on to college or the workforce. It's not an awful question, but answering it will not necessarily give you the outcome you may desire. When responding to that question at a young age, many folks give common answers like: "I want to be a Lawyer, a Doctor, or an Engineer.", but I learned a long time ago of a better question to ask yourself. And that is: "How do you want to live?" and "What type of lifestyle or business are you trying to create?"

That question opens up an entirely different point of view. It creates a discussion far superior to just asking yourself what you want to do when you grow up. It puts your thinking on a different trajectory which may require you to ask yourself further tough questions and devise a game plan for your future. I suggest figuring out how you want to live and work in reverse. Figure out your desired end goal for your business and work backward.

All too often, I have conversations with folks starting a lawn and landscaping business or who are looking to grow as they reach year two or three, and inevitably I hear the exact phrase out of almost everyone. They all say something along the lines of: "Next year, I'm going to get 50 new customers!" or "I will grow my business by $100k in revenue!" Not one to burst anyone's bubble or dash their dream, but my honest assessment is always: "But why?" "Why fifty new customers?" "Why $100k in new revenue?" "What is the reason for it?" Those are entirely arbitrary goals, and once you press in and ask the hard questions you realize that usually, they don't have any merit or stand on their own feet.

You see, all too often, people start a business of their own and before they know it, they get caught up in the habit and routine of growing to grow. There's no rhyme or reason, no strategy behind it, no game plan, and, you guessed it, no exit strategy. The conversations are constantly that of "I need to get new customers!" and "Next year, I'm going to crush it!". Statements like these can be a recipe for disaster. Your plans should be written out, quantified, measured, and distilled into precisely what they mean. I'm all for ambitious goals, but let's begin with why. Why are you trying to get fifty new customers? Why are you trying to grow your revenue by $100k? There has to be more to it than a feel-good answer.

As you start your business take ten to fifteen minutes and ask yourself what you want your business to look like. What does success look like for me? What would make me happy and what is something that I would consider successful? What income level am I looking to reach to provide the lifestyle I need for my family? How much money do I need to make to get there and what type of business, clientele, and infrastructure do I need to build to reach that goal? Asking these questions can be an exciting thought exercise that I promise you 98% of your peers, coworkers, friends, or family will never stop to engage in. The old saying goes that most people spend more time planning a two-week vacation than they do their entire financial lives, and I believe it!

The point of this conversation is this: What business are you looking to build? What are you trying to accomplish with this new endeavor? Don't get in the habit of just going through the motions, because, here's why: without a concrete vision for your future, when it gets challenging (and believe me, it will get challenging), you may end up throwing in the towel and hanging it up. I've seen so many people quit their businesses before they ever had a chance to succeed. Life took them out, circumstances got the best of them, and the dream of their own business just couldn't be sustained. In short, they became a statistic; after all, nine out of ten companies fail in their first five years, and nine out of those ten fail by their tenth year in business. The odds, unfortunately, are stacked against you, so what are you going to do to give yourself the best chance of success? Listen to me - it has very little to do with what trimmer, mower, truck, or marketing campaign you purchase! It has much more to do with the vision, dream, and grit to see it through!

Lawn care can be a rewarding and profitable career, but you have to see it through. In the beginning, it's going to be challenging. There will be a lot of pumping the brakes, cutting your teeth, and getting your feet wet. Welcome to the jungle; we've all been there! Entrepreneurship is learned by doing, not simply reading and studying. Take the game plan and outline we've laid out, add your flavor to the mix, and execute. Your new venture is hardly a proposition of "What do you want to do?" To me, it's an opportunity to answer the question: "How do you want to live?" That's what a business of yours can do for you. Now, you need to make it happen.

Chapter Eighteen

# A Community Like No Other

Many people will often say that entrepreneurship is one of the loneliest things you will ever do. I agree with that statement; there's some truth to it for sure. Running your own business can sometimes be daunting, overwhelming, and frustrating. We've all been there! Sometimes you're in the thick of it wondering am I going insane? Is anyone else dealing with the same crap that I am? It's hard to describe that feeling of being in the desert, but I promise you, you will inevitably go through it. Here's the kicker, you don't have to go at it alone.

Over the last fifteen years that I've been in business for myself in the green industry, we've always had someone to help us along the way. Some people were in my life for a year and other mentors for a few years. Some of my best friends have been with me for over a decade. "Everyone is in your life for a season, for a reason." as my friend Paul says. That is true. You see, along the way, I've had many people help me to become a better business owner, leader, and member of my community. At times, I've had some people put their arms around me and help to get my head straight. Thank God for those people!

One of the most incredible things about the green industry is the people - I promise you that. They're a breed like no other. They understand work ethic, commitment, and grit. They're not afraid to work, get dirty, lose some sleep, and put in the hours. The lawn and landscaping industry has some of the best and brightest people I've ever seen, which goes double for the social media community. We've met some incredible people in my quest to share my story and pour out the best we can to pay it forward on social media. Some of these people have turned into new best friends; folks I never would've met without the power of the internet.

When you started your business, maybe you knew but perhaps you didn't, that an entire community of like-minded independent thinkers believes the same way you do about your lawn care business! Call them crazy, call them committed, call them whatever you like, but they're some of the most incredible people I've ever gotten to know. There are many opportunities to network with people in the green industry at trade shows, live events, YouTube, and so much more. The industry is on the boom, big time, and the social aspect of the community is second to none. My biggest suggestion: plug in and get involved in the industry. Between the events and training that can help you grow, there's nothing like being around like-minded people that think and believe the same way you do. Entrepreneurship can be lonely but it doesn't have to be when you have a community like ours.

## Chapter Nineteen

# Nike Said It Best

I often think to myself what an incredible journey it's been these last fifteen years and what if we had never gotten started with our lawn care business? I know it may not seem very serious, but as I look back on it, I can't imagine my life unfolding any other way. This adventure has been truly unforgettable and I often think quietly to myself, Thank God we acted. Thank God we went out a limb and gave it a try. Thank God we didn't wait for all the stoplights to turn green before we started. You often hear people suggesting getting your ducks in a row, but I will say this, I've never seen a row of ducks in a perfect line crossing the street, not ever!

The difference between those who achieve and those who think about it is one word: execution. You can watch endless TED talks and motivational YouTube videos all you want, but you have to do the thing at the end of the day. The part that is so hard to express in this book is the doing. It's the phone calls, the networking, and the business building that is where the real magic happens. I know people, just like you do, that are constantly "getting ready to get ready" and can never make a quality decision for the life of them. Ask them what the delay is and they will rebuttal with "I just need a little more time or more info." There's a balance between knowing everything and knowing enough to make a quality decision. Once you have about 80% of the information needed to decide, the next step is to act.

Nike said it best, "Just do it." The difference between those who pick up this book and do nothing and those who build the next multi-million dollar business (if you so choose!) is this: action. That's it! I challenge you to set a goal, get a game plan, forget the goal, and work the plan. You'd be surprised what you can do in a few short years if you let yourself go for it! Hey, we're not the sharpest knives in the drawer, and we still made it work! I know you can too. Thousands have before you, thousands will after you, so why not you, and why not now? You can do it, I believe in you big time, and you can make this industry a career and build a great business. Now go, and make it happen!

# Acknowledgments

I want to acknowledge a handful of folks who have made this journey unforgettable. The entrepreneurial journey has some of the highs, lows, and even loops that can make it an incredible rollecoaster. Sometimes you know the people on the roller coaster with you and sometimes you make new friends by the time the ride is over. Here's to some new friends that I've made along the way.

Thank you to Paul Jamison, a dear friend and an encourager like no other. Without him, this book would never have been more than another one of my crazy ideas on a never-ending to-do list. Paul is that friend that makes you want to be better and to do better. Without Paul, there would be no podcast, no books, and a much duller Brian Fullerton. Iron truly does sharpen iron. I appreciate your friendship, Paul.

A special thanks to Keith Kalfas. Keith not only helped me to get my message out there but he also believed in me until I believed in myself. Keith taught me how to share that message. His fingerprints are on every person we've blessed with our content. Keith is a rare breed. I'll be forever indebted to him. Love you, Keith.

I also want to thank Stanley Genadek (The Dirt Monkey) for his fatherly presence and encouragement. Stan was with me during some of the most challenging years while building my YouTube channel. I remember when I wanted to quit almost daily during our second and third years of YouTube. Stan was there to make sure we didn't give up. Without his strength, encouragement, quirky sense of humor, and unwavering belief in what we were putting together, we would've died on the vine, no doubt about it. Thank you, Stan.

Additionally, I would like to thank Bryan Race for your steadfast commitment, wisdom, and wise counsel over the years. With your help, we've shared our message (unfiltered) with more people than we ever imagined. Words cannot express how thankful I am for your partnership and friendship over these last few years. You have blessed so many and I don't think you'll ever know your full impact on their lives. I cannot wait to see where your future takes you.

I couldn't finish this book without acknowledging one last friend (although I could mention many more) who has seen it all unfold. Michael Bedell has been with me during the good, the bad, and even the ugly. It was a fateful meeting when Mike and I met back in 2016; we often joke about who saved who. Michael had just gone through a rough patch in his business. I was rebuilding my company and desperately needed business coaching. The two unlikeliest people to make new friends ended up striking up a conversation, and the rest, they say, is history. Michael helped me lay the foundation of my business and got me on two feet over the next few years. Every subsequent phone call and lunch meeting quickly went on for hours, and I'll never forget them. Michael's fellowship, encouragement, and steadfastness as a true friend are something you don't see much of anymore. Words can never describe how much you've done for my family. I'll never be able to repay you. Thank you for all of your friendship and wisdom over the years. You are a fantastic friend and will go down as one of the greats in our industry.

Last but not least, thank you to my beautiful wife, Elizabeth Fullerton. I would be nothing without you; that's a fact. No matter the struggle or challenge, we've been there together every step of the way. It's wild to see what we've been through this last decade together, and I can only imagine what the future holds over the next several decades. As unpredictable as it all may be, the one thing I can always count on is that we'll be together every step of the way. Thank you for always believing in me and joining me on this wild adventure. Together together. Forever forever! I Love You.

www.ingramcontent.com/pod-product-compliance
Lightning Source LLC
Chambersburg PA
CBHW072206090426
42740CB00012B/2416